DISCARD

FIREFIGHTERS

by Meg Gaertner

Cody Koala

An Imprint of Pop!
popbooksonline.com

abdopublishing.com

Published by Pop!, a division of ABDO, PO Box 398166, Minneapolis, Minnesota 55439. Copyright © 2019 by POP, LLC. International copyrights reserved in all countries. No part of this book may be reproduced in any form without written permission from the publisher. Pop!™ is a trademark and logo of POP, LLC.

Printed in the United States of America, North Mankato, Minnesota

042018
092018

THIS BOOK CONTAINS RECYCLED MATERIALS

Cover Photo: Shutterstock Images
Interior Photos: Shutterstock Images, 1, 5 (top), 5 (bottom left), 6, 13 (top), 13 (bottom right), 14–15, 17, 19 (top), 19 (bottom left), 20; Nate Billings/The Oklahoman/AP Images, 5 (bottom right); iStockphoto, 9, 10, 13 (bottom left), 16, 19 (bottom right)

Editor: Charly Haley
Series Designer: Laura Mitchell

Library of Congress Control Number: 2017963375

Publisher's Cataloging-in-Publication Data

Names: Gaertner, Meg, author.
Title: Firefighters / by Meg Gaertner.
Description: Minneapolis, Minnesota : Pop!, 2019. | Series: Community workers | Includes online resources and index.
Identifiers: ISBN 9781532160110 (lib.bdg.) | ISBN 9781532161230 (ebook) |
Subjects: LCSH: Fire fighters--Juvenile literature. | Fire fighting--Juvenile literature. | Rescue work--Juvenile literature. | Occupations--Careers--Jobs--Juvenile literature. | Community life--Juvenile literature.
Classification: DDC 628.92--dc23

Hello! My name is

Cody Koala

Pop open this book and you'll find QR codes like this one, loaded with information, so you can learn even more!

Scan this code* and others like it while you read, or visit the website below to make this book pop.

popbooksonline.com/firefighters

*Scanning QR codes requires a web-enabled smart device with a QR code reader app and a camera.

Table of Contents

Chapter 1

A Day in the Life

A call comes in. Firefighters at the station jump up. They put on their gear. They get in their **fire engine**. They are ready to go put out a fire.

Watch a video here!

The firefighters might need to rescue someone from a burning building. They might give **first aid** to someone who is hurt.

Many calls to firefighters are false alarms. These calls are by mistake and are not real **emergencies**.

Chapter 2

The Work

Firefighters are on call for emergencies. They have to be ready in case someone needs help.

Firefighters can be on call for one or two days at a time.

Learn more here!

Most calls are not about fires. Most calls are from people who are hurt and need **medical** care. Firefighters treat people until they can go to a hospital in an **ambulance**.

Chapter 3

Tools for Firefighting

Special pants and coats guard firefighters from heat. Fire fills the air with smoke. Masks and air **tanks** give firefighters clean air to breathe.

Learn more here!

Fire engines carry the
tools firefighters need.
They have medical kits and

fire extinguishers. They have
ladders to help firefighters
climb into burning buildings.

Fire engines have huge
water tanks. The tanks
connect to hoses. The hoses
spray water on the fire.

Chapter 4

Helping the Community

Firefighters do not just put out fires and help people who are hurt. Firefighters also make sure buildings are safe. They teach people about fire safety.

Complete an activity here!

People know they can call firefighters when they are in need. Firefighters will help them.

Most firefighters are volunteers. They work for free. They want to help the community.

Making Connections

Text-to-Self

Have you ever met a firefighter? What did you think of him or her? Would you ever want to be a firefighter?

Text-to-Text

Have you read other books about community workers? How are their jobs different from a firefighter's?

Text-to-World

Bad fires are sometimes reported in the news. What have you seen about firefighters in the news?

Glossary

ambulance – a vehicle that gives people medical care while taking them to a hospital.

emergency – when something unsafe happens and needs to be fixed quickly.

fire engine – a special truck used by firefighters to carry their tools and fight fires.

fire extinguisher – a tool people use to put out fires with foam.

first aid – help for a person who is sick or hurt.

medical – having to do with doctors or medicine.

tank – a large holder for gas or liquids.

Index

Online Resources

popbooksonline.com

Thanks for reading this Cody Koala book!

Scan this code* and others like it in this book, or visit the website below to make this book pop!

popbooksonline.com/firefighters

*Scanning QR codes requires a web-enabled smart device with a QR code reader app and a camera.